JOURNAL

THE TOTAL MONEY MAKEOVER

JOURNAL

DAVE RAMSEY

NELSON
BOOKS

An Imprint of Thomas Nelson

Published in Nashville, Tennessee, by Nelson Books, an imprint of Thomas Nelson. Nelson Books and Thomas Nelson are registered trademarks of HarperCollins Christian Publishing, Inc.

Thomas Nelson titles may be purchased in bulk for educational, business, fund-raising, or sales promotional use. For information, please e-mail SpecialMarkets@ ThomasNelson.com.

Scripture quotations marked KJV are from the King James Version. Public domain.

Scripture quotations marked NIV are from the Holy Bible, New International Version®, NIV®. Copyright © 1973, 1978, 1984, 2011 by Biblica, Inc.® Used by permission of Zondervan. All rights reserved worldwide. www.Zondervan.com. The "NIV" and "New International Version" are trademarks registered in the United States Patent and Trademark Office by Biblica, Inc.®

ISBN 978-1-4041-1007-6

Printed in China

19 20 21 22 23   RRD   10 9 8 7 6 5 4 3 2 1

"There is ultimately only one way to financial peace, and that is to walk daily with the Prince of Peace, Christ Jesus."

WHY JOURNAL?

I want to talk you into doing something you normally wouldn't do. I want you to track your progress through your Total Money Makeover in writing. Journaling this process in detail will be a huge tool and great treasure for you if you make the effort. I know that writing everything down as you go means more work, but the payoff will be well worth it.

Take this journal and record everything happening that seems like a big deal. Record the relationship issues, the debt, the emotions, the setbacks, the victories, and anything else that seems important at the time. Just so you know: I am not a big journaling nerd. But I did this through my process of going broke and losing everything. While you are heading the other direction with your Total Money Makeover, you will likely get the same benefits I got by journaling.

The immediate benefits of writing everything down are twofold. First, writing helps you process the problems and victories. Have you ever had a problem and sat down with a friend for advice? We have all had the experience that by the time we finished describing the problem, we knew the answer. The reason that we answered our own question is that in order to verbalize the problem we converted our jumbled thoughts to concise ideas that clarified the situation. The same thing happens when you write out the "crisis of the day" or—hopefully more often than not—your latest victory. This new clarity will help you move faster through your Total Money Makeover.

The second immediate benefit of journaling is that you can reread your entry just days—even months—later and gain vital perspective on your progress. When we were going broke, I remember entering a very emotional, hopeless entry. It was right after we lost one of our apartment complexes to foreclosure. "Gloom, despair, and agony on me. . . ." It sounded like a *Hee Haw* song. My entry pretty much revealed how I knew life on the planet was over, thanks to this particular foreclosure. Of course, it wasn't. The weird thing is that just a few weeks later, while still heading toward bankruptcy, I reread my entry and laughed. Rereading my hopeless entry didn't depress me; it gave me perspective. I realized that life on the planet hadn't ended, so maybe—just maybe—I was being a little melodramatic. This isn't to devalue the feelings I had in the middle of the crisis, but to highlight the fact that the next time I faced a "planet-ending crisis," I was better prepared, emotionally and spiritually. Journaling helps you see the big picture during your Total Money Makeover.

But I think possibly the best reason to do this journal is that it makes a generational gift. I have a copy of my great-great-grandfather's memoirs. He fought in the Civil War, later founded a college, and even later became a preacher. The memoirs are full of challenges, humor, and wonderful stories. If you leave this book to your great-great-grandchildren, full of what you experienced while having your Total Money Makeover, you will have left a real treasure.

I believe that if you do with money what we teach, then you will literally be able to financially change your family tree. I think it would be very cool to leave this journal to document how you did it. So here is my challenge:

Write it down.

You will be glad you did.

—DAVE RAMSEY

DATE 3/13/24   _____ DAYS WITH A WIN!

– check dposit

– pay credit card

TODAY'S GOALS

_____ ☐ SUCCESS!

_____ ☐ SUCCESS!

_____ ☐ SUCCESS!

_____ ☐ SUCCESS!

NEEDS WORK	REASONS TO KEEP GOING

DATE _____

"You can't spend your way out of guilt."

TODAY'S GOALS

_____ ☐ SUCCESS!

_____ ☐ SUCCESS!

_____ ☐ SUCCESS!

_____ ☐ SUCCESS!

NEEDS WORK

REASONS TO KEEP GOING

DATE _____

Federal Tax 2023.
—need to pay

> "Money can be
> the light that
> exposes wounds
> or other problems
> in the midst of a
> volatile setting."

TODAY'S GOALS

_____ ☐ SUCCESS!

_____ ☐ SUCCESS!

_____ ☐ SUCCESS!

_____ ☐ SUCCESS!

NEEDS WORK

REASONS TO KEEP GOING

DATE _____

"How you handle
or mishandle
your money
tells us who you
are, and, more
important, it tells
you who you are."

TODAY'S GOALS

_____ ☐ SUCCESS!

_____ ☐ SUCCESS!

_____ ☐ SUCCESS!

_____ ☐ SUCCESS!

NEEDS WORK	REASONS TO KEEP GOING

DATE _____

> "The understanding that the wealth is really God's, and you are managing it not only for yourself, but also for the good of others, frees you."

TODAY'S GOALS

_____ ☐ SUCCESS!

_____ ☐ SUCCESS!

_____ ☐ SUCCESS!

_____ ☐ SUCCESS!

NEEDS WORK	REASONS TO KEEP GOING

DATE _____

_____ **DAYS WITH A WIN!**

"Do the things
that are
important in
ways that are
noble, and you
will be led to *More
Than Enough*."

TODAY'S GOALS

_____ ☐ SUCCESS!

_____ ☐ SUCCESS!

_____ ☐ SUCCESS!

_____ ☐ SUCCESS!

NEEDS WORK

REASONS TO KEEP GOING

"Remember, you can't teach your children to work unless you do."

TODAY'S GOALS

_____ ☐ SUCCESS!

_____ ☐ SUCCESS!

_____ ☐ SUCCESS!

_____ ☐ SUCCESS!

NEEDS WORK

REASONS TO KEEP GOING

DATE _____

"Your priorities, passions, goals, and fears are shown clearly in the flow of your money."

TODAY'S GOALS

_____ ☐ SUCCESS!

_____ ☐ SUCCESS!

_____ ☐ SUCCESS!

_____ ☐ SUCCESS!

NEEDS WORK

REASONS TO KEEP GOING

DATE _____

> "Vision that is rooted in values is the only vision that will last."

TODAY'S GOALS

_____ ☐ SUCCESS!

_____ ☐ SUCCESS!

_____ ☐ SUCCESS!

_____ ☐ SUCCESS!

NEEDS WORK

REASONS TO KEEP GOING

DATE _____

_____ DAYS WITH A WIN!

"Goals are the practical building blocks that make a vision come true."

TODAY'S GOALS

_____ ☐ SUCCESS!

_____ ☐ SUCCESS!

_____ ☐ SUCCESS!

_____ ☐ SUCCESS!

NEEDS WORK

REASONS TO KEEP GOING

DATE _____

> "Courage always gets you dirty; you have to be in the middle of the action to create action."

TODAY'S GOALS

_____ ☐ SUCCESS!

_____ ☐ SUCCESS!

_____ ☐ SUCCESS!

_____ ☐ SUCCESS!

NEEDS WORK	REASONS TO KEEP GOING

DATE _____

"When money
is in your
possession, what
you do with it
screams loudly
who you are."

TODAY'S GOALS

_____ ☐ SUCCESS!

_____ ☐ SUCCESS!

_____ ☐ SUCCESS!

_____ ☐ SUCCESS!

NEEDS WORK

REASONS TO KEEP GOING

> "Problems give us the ability to hang on, and that ability changes who we are."

TODAY'S GOALS

_____ ☐ SUCCESS!

_____ ☐ SUCCESS!

_____ ☐ SUCCESS!

_____ ☐ SUCCESS!

NEEDS WORK

REASONS TO KEEP GOING

DATE _____ _____ DAYS WITH A WIN!

> "[S]orrow looks back, worry looks around, while faith looks up."
> ANONYMOUS

TODAY'S GOALS

_____ ☐ SUCCESS!

_____ ☐ SUCCESS!

_____ ☐ SUCCESS!

_____ ☐ SUCCESS!

NEEDS WORK

REASONS TO KEEP GOING

DATE _____   _____ DAYS WITH A WIN!

> "Don't allow failure to steal your hope."

TODAY'S GOALS

_____ ☐ SUCCESS!

_____ ☐ SUCCESS!

_____ ☐ SUCCESS!

_____ ☐ SUCCESS!

NEEDS WORK

REASONS TO KEEP GOING

DATE _____

"It isn't just
how we spend
money; it's also
how we handle
our finances
that marks us
as opposites."

TODAY'S GOALS

_____ ☐ SUCCESS!

_____ ☐ SUCCESS!

_____ ☐ SUCCESS!

_____ ☐ SUCCESS!

NEEDS WORK

REASONS TO KEEP GOING

DATE _____

> "The past can hurt, but you can either run from it or learn from it."
> **RAFIKI IN**
> *THE LION KING*

TODAY'S GOALS

_____ ☐ SUCCESS!

_____ ☐ SUCCESS!

_____ ☐ SUCCESS!

_____ ☐ SUCCESS!

NEEDS WORK

REASONS TO KEEP GOING

"The power of being connected to people pulling the same way adds insight, ingenuity, ideas, values, energy, and good habits that can mushroom."

TODAY'S GOALS

_____ ☐ SUCCESS!

_____ ☐ SUCCESS!

_____ ☐ SUCCESS!

_____ ☐ SUCCESS!

NEEDS WORK

REASONS TO KEEP GOING

DATE _____

_____ DAYS WITH A WIN!

> "Criticize a man
> in financial
> difficulty, and you
> will see instant
> and dramatic
> flight or fight."

TODAY'S GOALS

_____ ☐ SUCCESS!

_____ ☐ SUCCESS!

_____ ☐ SUCCESS!

_____ ☐ SUCCESS!

NEEDS WORK	REASONS TO KEEP GOING

"When life ties you up and throws you in a pit, you have to make choices. You have to decide what to do at the bottom."

TODAY'S GOALS

_____ ☐ SUCCESS!

_____ ☐ SUCCESS!

_____ ☐ SUCCESS!

_____ ☐ SUCCESS!

NEEDS WORK

REASONS TO KEEP GOING

DATE _____

> "Cowards can never be moral."
> MAHATMA GANDHI

TODAY'S GOALS

_____ ☐ SUCCESS!

_____ ☐ SUCCESS!

_____ ☐ SUCCESS!

_____ ☐ SUCCESS!

NEEDS WORK	REASONS TO KEEP GOING

"The most powerful form of behavior modification is the properly run small group."

TODAY'S GOALS

_____ ☐ SUCCESS!

_____ ☐ SUCCESS!

_____ ☐ SUCCESS!

_____ ☐ SUCCESS!

NEEDS WORK	REASONS TO KEEP GOING

DATE _____

"Intensity is a
key ingredient
in the lives of
people who win."

TODAY'S GOALS

_____ ☐ SUCCESS!

_____ ☐ SUCCESS!

_____ ☐ SUCCESS!

_____ ☐ SUCCESS!

NEEDS WORK	REASONS TO KEEP GOING

DATE _____

"Some folks have their feet planted firmly on the ground and move like it. Other folks understand or at least have a glimpse of the power of momentum."

TODAY'S GOALS

_____ ☐ SUCCESS!

_____ ☐ SUCCESS!

_____ ☐ SUCCESS!

_____ ☐ SUCCESS!

NEEDS WORK

REASONS TO KEEP GOING

"[T]he bulk of the blame [for this credit excess] lies with the character represented in our financial institutions and their decision makers."

TODAY'S GOALS

_____ ☐ SUCCESS!

_____ ☐ SUCCESS!

_____ ☐ SUCCESS!

_____ ☐ SUCCESS!

NEEDS WORK

REASONS TO KEEP GOING

> "Concentration:
> put all your eggs
> in one basket and
> watch that basket."
> **DALE CARNEGIE**

TODAY'S GOALS

_____ ☐ SUCCESS!

_____ ☐ SUCCESS!

_____ ☐ SUCCESS!

_____ ☐ SUCCESS!

NEEDS WORK	REASONS TO KEEP GOING

DATE _____

> "Prayer is vital, but God is not in the business of rewarding the lazy."

TODAY'S GOALS

_____ ☐ SUCCESS!

_____ ☐ SUCCESS!

_____ ☐ SUCCESS!

_____ ☐ SUCCESS!

NEEDS WORK	REASONS TO KEEP GOING

"If you spend
your day looking
for easy work,
you will still go
to bed worn out."
ANONYMOUS

TODAY'S GOALS

_____ ☐ SUCCESS!

_____ ☐ SUCCESS!

_____ ☐ SUCCESS!

_____ ☐ SUCCESS!

NEEDS WORK

REASONS TO KEEP GOING

DATE _____

> "The habits, character traits, and abilities that make someone able to build wealth also make him able to manage it."

TODAY'S GOALS

_____ ☐ SUCCESS!

_____ ☐ SUCCESS!

_____ ☐ SUCCESS!

_____ ☐ SUCCESS!

NEEDS WORK

REASONS TO KEEP GOING

DATE _____

> "Those who have
> never made a
> mistake usually
> work for those
> who have."
> **HENRY FORD**

TODAY'S GOALS

_____ ☐ SUCCESS!

_____ ☐ SUCCESS!

_____ ☐ SUCCESS!

_____ ☐ SUCCESS!

NEEDS WORK

REASONS TO KEEP GOING

DATE _____

> "You cannot have healthy relationships and build wealth with lies as your foundation."

TODAY'S GOALS

_____ ☐ SUCCESS!

_____ ☐ SUCCESS!

_____ ☐ SUCCESS!

_____ ☐ SUCCESS!

NEEDS WORK	REASONS TO KEEP GOING

> "I have never been poor, only broke. Being poor is a frame of mind."
>
> MIKE TODD

TODAY'S GOALS

_____ ☐ SUCCESS!

_____ ☐ SUCCESS!

_____ ☐ SUCCESS!

_____ ☐ SUCCESS!

NEEDS WORK

REASONS TO KEEP GOING

DATE _____   _____ DAYS WITH A WIN!

> "The problem with the clenched-fist money-management style is that while those dollars can't get away, new dollars can't get in, either."

TODAY'S GOALS

_____ ☐ SUCCESS!
_____ ☐ SUCCESS!
_____ ☐ SUCCESS!
_____ ☐ SUCCESS!

NEEDS WORK	REASONS TO KEEP GOING

DATE _____

"Nature gave us two ends—one to sit on and one to think with. Ever since then man's success or failure has been dependent on which one he used most."

GEORGE KIRKPATRICK

TODAY'S GOALS

_____ ☐ SUCCESS!

_____ ☐ SUCCESS!

_____ ☐ SUCCESS!

_____ ☐ SUCCESS!

NEEDS WORK	REASONS TO KEEP GOING

DATE _____ _____ DAYS WITH A WIN!

> "No discipline
> seems pleasant
> at the time, but
> painful. Later
> on, however, it
> produces a harvest
> of righteousness
> and peace for those
> who have been
> trained by it."
> HEBREWS 12:11 (NIV)

TODAY'S GOALS

_____ ☐ SUCCESS!

_____ ☐ SUCCESS!

_____ ☐ SUCCESS!

_____ ☐ SUCCESS!

NEEDS WORK	REASONS TO KEEP GOING

DATE _____   _____ DAYS WITH A WIN!

> "The more mature you are, the longer you can wait for the satisfaction that completion brings."

TODAY'S GOALS

_____ ☐ SUCCESS!

_____ ☐ SUCCESS!

_____ ☐ SUCCESS!

_____ ☐ SUCCESS!

NEEDS WORK

REASONS TO KEEP GOING

DATE _____

> "When you learn to respect others—adults *and* children—you will see yourself improve in self-esteem, happiness, and fulfillment."
>
> SHARON RAMSEY

TODAY'S GOALS

_____ ☐ SUCCESS!

_____ ☐ SUCCESS!

_____ ☐ SUCCESS!

_____ ☐ SUCCESS!

NEEDS WORK

REASONS TO KEEP GOING

DATE _____

> "Far and away the best prize that life offers is the chance to work hard at work worth doing."
> **TEDDY ROOSEVELT**

TODAY'S GOALS

_____ ☐ SUCCESS!

_____ ☐ SUCCESS!

_____ ☐ SUCCESS!

_____ ☐ SUCCESS!

NEEDS WORK

REASONS TO KEEP GOING

> "When you give, passion, joy, and intensity come to you like waves crashing at the seashore."

TODAY'S GOALS

_____ ☐ SUCCESS!

_____ ☐ SUCCESS!

_____ ☐ SUCCESS!

_____ ☐ SUCCESS!

NEEDS WORK

REASONS TO KEEP GOING

DATE _____

> "I do not know anyone who has gotten to the top without hard work."
> MARGARET THATCHER

TODAY'S GOALS

_____ ☐ SUCCESS!

_____ ☐ SUCCESS!

_____ ☐ SUCCESS!

_____ ☐ SUCCESS!

NEEDS WORK

REASONS TO KEEP GOING

DATE _____

> "If you give because you think that makes God owe you a favor and you are promised to get more, you will mess up the whole process."

TODAY'S GOALS

_____ ☐ SUCCESS!

_____ ☐ SUCCESS!

_____ ☐ SUCCESS!

_____ ☐ SUCCESS!

NEEDS WORK

REASONS TO KEEP GOING

> "[M]oney is just the method that the Great Teacher has chosen to expose and correct our flaws as well as give us 'attaboys' for a job well done."

TODAY'S GOALS

_____ ☐ SUCCESS!

_____ ☐ SUCCESS!

_____ ☐ SUCCESS!

_____ ☐ SUCCESS!

NEEDS WORK

REASONS TO KEEP GOING

DATE _____   _____ DAYS WITH A WIN!

TODAY'S GOALS

_____ ☐ SUCCESS!

_____ ☐ SUCCESS!

_____ ☐ SUCCESS!

_____ ☐ SUCCESS!

NEEDS WORK

REASONS TO KEEP GOING

_____ DAYS WITH A WIN!

"I have found that
the best way to
handle money
properly is to
trick yourself
into it."

TODAY'S GOALS

_____ ☐ SUCCESS!

_____ ☐ SUCCESS!

_____ ☐ SUCCESS!

_____ ☐ SUCCESS!

NEEDS WORK	REASONS TO KEEP GOING

DATE _____   _____ DAYS WITH A WIN!

> "Do not attempt to
> do a thing unless you
> are sure of yourself;
> but do not relinquish
> it simply because
> someone else is
> not sure of you."
> STEWART WHITE

TODAY'S GOALS

_____ ☐ SUCCESS!

_____ ☐ SUCCESS!

_____ ☐ SUCCESS!

_____ ☐ SUCCESS!

NEEDS WORK	REASONS TO KEEP GOING

DATE _____

> "If a man hasn't discovered something that he will die for, he isn't fit to live."
>
> DR. MARTIN LUTHER KING, JR.

TODAY'S GOALS

_____ ☐ SUCCESS!

_____ ☐ SUCCESS!

_____ ☐ SUCCESS!

_____ ☐ SUCCESS!

NEEDS WORK	REASONS TO KEEP GOING

DATE _____ _____ DAYS WITH A WIN!

> "There can be no money secrets from someone you are serious enough about to marry."

TODAY'S GOALS

_____ ☐ SUCCESS!

_____ ☐ SUCCESS!

_____ ☐ SUCCESS!

_____ ☐ SUCCESS!

NEEDS WORK

REASONS TO KEEP GOING

> "I'm a great believer in luck, and the harder I work the more I have of it."
> THOMAS JEFFERSON

TODAY'S GOALS

_____ ☐ SUCCESS!

_____ ☐ SUCCESS!

_____ ☐ SUCCESS!

_____ ☐ SUCCESS!

NEEDS WORK

REASONS TO KEEP GOING

DATE _____   _____ DAYS WITH A WIN!

> "Hope is the powerful fuel that causes the engine of your life to develop all the horsepower it was designed to have."

TODAY'S GOALS

_____ ☐ SUCCESS!

_____ ☐ SUCCESS!

_____ ☐ SUCCESS!

_____ ☐ SUCCESS!

NEEDS WORK	REASONS TO KEEP GOING

"There is an old Danish proverb that says if you give a child everything he wants when he cries and a pig everything he wants when he grunts you will have a fine pig and a sorry child."

TODAY'S GOALS

_____ ☐ SUCCESS!

_____ ☐ SUCCESS!

_____ ☐ SUCCESS!

_____ ☐ SUCCESS!

NEEDS WORK

REASONS TO KEEP GOING

DATE _____   _____ DAYS WITH A WIN!

"... [T]he most important decision in achieving a goal is not what you are willing to do to achieve it, but what you are willing to give up to achieve it."
EARL NIGHTINGALE

TODAY'S GOALS

_____ ☐ SUCCESS!

_____ ☐ SUCCESS!

_____ ☐ SUCCESS!

_____ ☐ SUCCESS!

NEEDS WORK	REASONS TO KEEP GOING

DATE _____   _____ DAYS WITH A WIN!

> "Failure is natural, normal, and is going to happen."

TODAY'S GOALS

_____ ☐ SUCCESS!

_____ ☐ SUCCESS!

_____ ☐ SUCCESS!

_____ ☐ SUCCESS!

NEEDS WORK	REASONS TO KEEP GOING

DATE _____   _____ DAYS WITH A WIN!

> "Not all the wealthy
> are wise, but usually
> the wise will become
> wealthy given time."

TODAY'S GOALS

_____ ☐ SUCCESS!

_____ ☐ SUCCESS!

_____ ☐ SUCCESS!

_____ ☐ SUCCESS!

NEEDS WORK

REASONS TO KEEP GOING

DATE _____ _____ DAYS WITH A WIN!

"Marriage doesn't mean you lose your identity or competence; it does mean you have brought someone into your life you would die for. You have to die, alright—die to self."

TODAY'S GOALS

_____ ☐ SUCCESS!

_____ ☐ SUCCESS!

_____ ☐ SUCCESS!

_____ ☐ SUCCESS!

NEEDS WORK

REASONS TO KEEP GOING

DATE _____   _____ DAYS WITH A WIN!

> "Quiet strength
> is to wear
> power lightly,
> understanding that
> power is just like
> money—it is only a
> tool to help others."

TODAY'S GOALS

_____ ☐ SUCCESS!

_____ ☐ SUCCESS!

_____ ☐ SUCCESS!

_____ ☐ SUCCESS!

NEEDS WORK	REASONS TO KEEP GOING

"It is much
better to look
where you are
going than to
see where you
have been."

TODAY'S GOALS

_____ ☐ SUCCESS!

_____ ☐ SUCCESS!

_____ ☐ SUCCESS!

_____ ☐ SUCCESS!

NEEDS WORK

REASONS TO KEEP GOING

DATE _____

> "Meekness is not weakness; it is power under control."
> WARREN WIERSBE

TODAY'S GOALS

_____ ☐ SUCCESS!

_____ ☐ SUCCESS!

_____ ☐ SUCCESS!

_____ ☐ SUCCESS!

NEEDS WORK

REASONS TO KEEP GOING

"...[H]ope is the core of what makes people become what God designed them to be."

TODAY'S GOALS

_____ ☐ SUCCESS!

_____ ☐ SUCCESS!

_____ ☐ SUCCESS!

_____ ☐ SUCCESS!

NEEDS WORK

REASONS TO KEEP GOING

DATE _____

> "In an age when all our answers and information come in sound bites, we have lost an understanding of working through a process. And even more critically, we have lost the understanding of what true wisdom is."

TODAY'S GOALS

_____ ☐ SUCCESS!

_____ ☐ SUCCESS!

_____ ☐ SUCCESS!

_____ ☐ SUCCESS!

NEEDS WORK	REASONS TO KEEP GOING

DATE _____

_____ DAYS WITH A WIN!

"Courage seems
to be something
that is not talked
about anymore."

TODAY'S GOALS

_____ ☐ SUCCESS!

_____ ☐ SUCCESS!

_____ ☐ SUCCESS!

_____ ☐ SUCCESS!

NEEDS WORK

REASONS TO KEEP GOING

DATE _____

> "Even though talking might be hard ... communication will save your marriage."

TODAY'S GOALS

_____ ☐ SUCCESS!

_____ ☐ SUCCESS!

_____ ☐ SUCCESS!

_____ ☐ SUCCESS!

NEEDS WORK

REASONS TO KEEP GOING

DATE _____ _____ DAYS WITH A WIN!

"Giving works
because it is your
personal blueprint
to be a giver . . ."

TODAY'S GOALS

_____ ☐ SUCCESS!

_____ ☐ SUCCESS!

_____ ☐ SUCCESS!

_____ ☐ SUCCESS!

NEEDS WORK

REASONS TO KEEP GOING

> "Failure is the opportunity to begin again more intelligently."
> HENRY FORD

TODAY'S GOALS

_____ ☐ SUCCESS!

_____ ☐ SUCCESS!

_____ ☐ SUCCESS!

_____ ☐ SUCCESS!

NEEDS WORK	REASONS TO KEEP GOING

"[C]hildren have never been very good at listening to their elders, but they have never failed to imitate them."

JAMES BALDWIN

TODAY'S GOALS

_____ ☐ SUCCESS!

_____ ☐ SUCCESS!

_____ ☐ SUCCESS!

_____ ☐ SUCCESS!

NEEDS WORK

REASONS TO KEEP GOING

DATE _____

_____ DAYS WITH A WIN!

"If we take all the
lessons learned
from failure and
stack them [up] we
can easily get the
breathtaking view
that hope gives."

TODAY'S GOALS

_____ ☐ SUCCESS!

_____ ☐ SUCCESS!

_____ ☐ SUCCESS!

_____ ☐ SUCCESS!

NEEDS WORK

REASONS TO KEEP GOING

"Your compass is your values; they lead you to the road, which is vision, and you are able to find your way using the road signs, called goals."

TODAY'S GOALS

_____ ☐ SUCCESS!

_____ ☐ SUCCESS!

_____ ☐ SUCCESS!

_____ ☐ SUCCESS!

NEEDS WORK

REASONS TO KEEP GOING

DATE _____

> "Deception equals destruction."

TODAY'S GOALS

_____ ☐ SUCCESS!

_____ ☐ SUCCESS!

_____ ☐ SUCCESS!

_____ ☐ SUCCESS!

NEEDS WORK	REASONS TO KEEP GOING

> "In a culture that seems to give respect to loudmouths, we seem to have labeled those with quiet strength as weak."

TODAY'S GOALS

_____ ☐ SUCCESS!

_____ ☐ SUCCESS!

_____ ☐ SUCCESS!

_____ ☐ SUCCESS!

NEEDS WORK	REASONS TO KEEP GOING

> "Men and women are limited not by their intelligence, nor by their education, nor by the color of their skin, but by the size of their hope."
>
> **JOHN JOHNSON**

TODAY'S GOALS

_____ ☐ SUCCESS!

_____ ☐ SUCCESS!

_____ ☐ SUCCESS!

_____ ☐ SUCCESS!

NEEDS WORK

REASONS TO KEEP GOING

DATE _____

"Diligence . . .
comes with a
guarantee."

TODAY'S GOALS

_____ ☐ SUCCESS!

_____ ☐ SUCCESS!

_____ ☐ SUCCESS!

_____ ☐ SUCCESS!

NEEDS WORK	REASONS TO KEEP GOING

DATE _____ _____ DAYS WITH A WIN!

> "Prosperity may be a bigger test than poverty when it comes to exposing your weaknesses."

TODAY'S GOALS

_____ ☐ SUCCESS!

_____ ☐ SUCCESS!

_____ ☐ SUCCESS!

_____ ☐ SUCCESS!

NEEDS WORK

REASONS TO KEEP GOING

DATE _____

> "Hope placed properly is one of the most powerful forces you will ever know."

TODAY'S GOALS

_____ ☐ SUCCESS!

_____ ☐ SUCCESS!

_____ ☐ SUCCESS!

_____ ☐ SUCCESS!

NEEDS WORK	REASONS TO KEEP GOING

DATE _____   _____ DAYS WITH A WIN!

> "Remember, hope
> is on your side
> as long as you
> keep it there."
> **SHARON RAMSEY**

TODAY'S GOALS

_____   ☐ SUCCESS!

_____   ☐ SUCCESS!

_____   ☐ SUCCESS!

_____   ☐ SUCCESS!

NEEDS WORK

REASONS TO KEEP GOING

DATE _____

_____ DAYS WITH A WIN!

"A safe harbor is where rest, repair, and the restocking of provisions occur so that we can sail again."

TODAY'S GOALS

_____ ☐ SUCCESS!

_____ ☐ SUCCESS!

_____ ☐ SUCCESS!

_____ ☐ SUCCESS!

NEEDS WORK

REASONS TO KEEP GOING

DATE _____   _____ DAYS WITH A WIN!

"If you want uncommon results you have to think and do things that are uncommon."

TODAY'S GOALS

_____ ☐ SUCCESS!

_____ ☐ SUCCESS!

_____ ☐ SUCCESS!

_____ ☐ SUCCESS!

NEEDS WORK	REASONS TO KEEP GOING

"There are no hopeless situations, only people who are hopeless about them."

DINAH SHORE

TODAY'S GOALS

_____ ☐ SUCCESS!

_____ ☐ SUCCESS!

_____ ☐ SUCCESS!

_____ ☐ SUCCESS!

NEEDS WORK

REASONS TO KEEP GOING

DATE _____

> "When a man refuses to act like a man, his wife will act like his mother."
> ED COLE

TODAY'S GOALS

_____ ☐ SUCCESS!

_____ ☐ SUCCESS!

_____ ☐ SUCCESS!

_____ ☐ SUCCESS!

NEEDS WORK	REASONS TO KEEP GOING

DATE _____

"Man must cease attributing his problems to his environment, and learn again to exercise his will, his personal responsibility."
ALBERT SCHWEITZER

TODAY'S GOALS

_____ ☐ SUCCESS!

_____ ☐ SUCCESS!

_____ ☐ SUCCESS!

_____ ☐ SUCCESS!

NEEDS WORK

REASONS TO KEEP GOING

> "The trouble with most of us is that we would rather be ruined by praise than saved by criticism."
> NORMAN VINCENT PEALE

TODAY'S GOALS

_____ ☐ SUCCESS!

_____ ☐ SUCCESS!

_____ ☐ SUCCESS!

_____ ☐ SUCCESS!

NEEDS WORK

REASONS TO KEEP GOING

DATE _____

"Personal finance
is 80 percent
behavior and only
20 percent head
knowledge."

TODAY'S GOALS

_____ ☐ SUCCESS!

_____ ☐ SUCCESS!

_____ ☐ SUCCESS!

_____ ☐ SUCCESS!

NEEDS WORK

REASONS TO KEEP GOING

DATE _____

> "The quality of a person's life is in direct proportion to their commitment to excellence, regardless of their chosen field of endeavor."
> **VINCE LOMBARDI**

TODAY'S GOALS

_____ ☐ SUCCESS!

_____ ☐ SUCCESS!

_____ ☐ SUCCESS!

_____ ☐ SUCCESS!

NEEDS WORK	REASONS TO KEEP GOING

DATE _____

> "When times are good and you are on a mountaintop in your life, you need to maximize your life and your wealth."

TODAY'S GOALS

_____ ☐ SUCCESS!

_____ ☐ SUCCESS!

_____ ☐ SUCCESS!

_____ ☐ SUCCESS!

NEEDS WORK

REASONS TO KEEP GOING

DATE _____ _____ DAYS WITH A WIN!

> "Intensity is a decision to attack, to have passion, and to purposefully put power into your thoughts and actions."

TODAY'S GOALS

_____ ☐ SUCCESS!

_____ ☐ SUCCESS!

_____ ☐ SUCCESS!

_____ ☐ SUCCESS!

NEEDS WORK	REASONS TO KEEP GOING

> "When the pain of *same* hurts so bad that we consider adjusting our behavior, the pain of *change* is just around the corner."

TODAY'S GOALS

_____ ☐ SUCCESS!

_____ ☐ SUCCESS!

_____ ☐ SUCCESS!

_____ ☐ SUCCESS!

NEEDS WORK

REASONS TO KEEP GOING

> "Those people who you are with for life are the ones who naturally lend themselves to holding you accountable and are the ones who will support you."

TODAY'S GOALS

_____ ☐ SUCCESS!

_____ ☐ SUCCESS!

_____ ☐ SUCCESS!

_____ ☐ SUCCESS!

NEEDS WORK	REASONS TO KEEP GOING

DATE _____   _____ DAYS WITH A WIN!

> "[Real courage] is courage that reflects values and stands firmly on them."

TODAY'S GOALS

_____ ☐ SUCCESS!

_____ ☐ SUCCESS!

_____ ☐ SUCCESS!

_____ ☐ SUCCESS!

NEEDS WORK	REASONS TO KEEP GOING

DATE _____

_____ DAYS WITH A WIN!

> "The first requirement of success is the ability to apply your physical and mental energies to one problem incessantly without growing weary."
> THOMAS EDISON

TODAY'S GOALS

_____ ☐ SUCCESS!

_____ ☐ SUCCESS!

_____ ☐ SUCCESS!

_____ ☐ SUCCESS!

NEEDS WORK

REASONS TO KEEP GOING

> "When you have contentment you can easily get out of debt."

TODAY'S GOALS

_____ ☐ SUCCESS!

_____ ☐ SUCCESS!

_____ ☐ SUCCESS!

_____ ☐ SUCCESS!

NEEDS WORK

REASONS TO KEEP GOING

DATE _____

> "People change their lives when they say 'I've had it!'"
> LES BROWN

TODAY'S GOALS

_____ ☐ SUCCESS!

_____ ☐ SUCCESS!

_____ ☐ SUCCESS!

_____ ☐ SUCCESS!

NEEDS WORK

REASONS TO KEEP GOING

DATE _____

_____ DAYS WITH A WIN!

> "[I]t is worth the trouble to become the person you know God made you to be."

TODAY'S GOALS

_____ ☐ SUCCESS!

_____ ☐ SUCCESS!

_____ ☐ SUCCESS!

_____ ☐ SUCCESS!

NEEDS WORK

REASONS TO KEEP GOING

DATE _____

> "People who don't give are stopped up. Things flow in but nothing flows out."

TODAY'S GOALS

_____ ☐ SUCCESS!

_____ ☐ SUCCESS!

_____ ☐ SUCCESS!

_____ ☐ SUCCESS!

NEEDS WORK	REASONS TO KEEP GOING

DATE _____

"Where there is no vision, the people perish."
PROVERBS 29:18 (KJV)

TODAY'S GOALS

_____ ☐ SUCCESS!

_____ ☐ SUCCESS!

_____ ☐ SUCCESS!

_____ ☐ SUCCESS!

NEEDS WORK

REASONS TO KEEP GOING

DATE _____

> "One of the most important gifts you can teach your children is the power of initiative. Move on it! Go get it!"

TODAY'S GOALS

_____ ☐ SUCCESS!

_____ ☐ SUCCESS!

_____ ☐ SUCCESS!

_____ ☐ SUCCESS!

NEEDS WORK	REASONS TO KEEP GOING

DATE _____

_____ DAYS WITH A WIN!

> "Backward momentum is as powerful and hard to stop as forward momentum."

TODAY'S GOALS

_____ ☐ SUCCESS!

_____ ☐ SUCCESS!

_____ ☐ SUCCESS!

_____ ☐ SUCCESS!

NEEDS WORK

REASONS TO KEEP GOING

DATE _____

"God asked
Solomon what
he wanted and
the answer was
wisdom."

TODAY'S GOALS

_____ ☐ SUCCESS!

_____ ☐ SUCCESS!

_____ ☐ SUCCESS!

_____ ☐ SUCCESS!

NEEDS WORK	REASONS TO KEEP GOING

DATE _____

"Money is a mirror that, strange as it sounds, reflects our personal strengths and weaknesses with amazing clarity."

TODAY'S GOALS

_____ ☐ SUCCESS!

_____ ☐ SUCCESS!

_____ ☐ SUCCESS!

_____ ☐ SUCCESS!

NEEDS WORK

REASONS TO KEEP GOING

DATE _____   _____ DAYS WITH A WIN!

"Ninety percent
of investing is
just doing it."

TODAY'S GOALS

_____   ☐ SUCCESS!

_____   ☐ SUCCESS!

_____   ☐ SUCCESS!

_____   ☐ SUCCESS!

NEEDS WORK	REASONS TO KEEP GOING

DATE _____

> "The pressure and drama that are created by silence born of patience will make you money in negotiations."

TODAY'S GOALS

_____ ☐ SUCCESS!

_____ ☐ SUCCESS!

_____ ☐ SUCCESS!

_____ ☐ SUCCESS!

NEEDS WORK

REASONS TO KEEP GOING

DATE _____   _____ DAYS WITH A WIN!

> "A get-rich-quick
> mentality has at its
> core a laziness."

TODAY'S GOALS

_____ ☐ SUCCESS!

_____ ☐ SUCCESS!

_____ ☐ SUCCESS!

_____ ☐ SUCCESS!

NEEDS WORK	REASONS TO KEEP GOING

DATE _____

"You aren't
anyone else's job."

TODAY'S GOALS

_____ ☐ SUCCESS!

_____ ☐ SUCCESS!

_____ ☐ SUCCESS!

_____ ☐ SUCCESS!

NEEDS WORK	REASONS TO KEEP GOING

DATE _____   _____ DAYS WITH A WIN!

"Hard work opens locked doors."

TODAY'S GOALS

_____ ☐ SUCCESS!

_____ ☐ SUCCESS!

_____ ☐ SUCCESS!

_____ ☐ SUCCESS!

NEEDS WORK	REASONS TO KEEP GOING

> "If you measure success in service, money will flow to you."

TODAY'S GOALS

_____ ☐ SUCCESS!

_____ ☐ SUCCESS!

_____ ☐ SUCCESS!

_____ ☐ SUCCESS!

NEEDS WORK	REASONS TO KEEP GOING

DATE _____   _____ DAYS WITH A WIN!

> "When one door closes, another opens; but we often look so long and so regretfully upon the closed door that we do not see the one which has opened for us."
> ALEXANDER GRAHAM BELL

TODAY'S GOALS

_____ ☐ SUCCESS!

_____ ☐ SUCCESS!

_____ ☐ SUCCESS!

_____ ☐ SUCCESS!

NEEDS WORK	REASONS TO KEEP GOING

DATE _____   _____ DAYS WITH A WIN!

"Our culture worships information, but information without application is an empty deity."
DENNIS RAINEY

TODAY'S GOALS

_____ ☐ SUCCESS!

_____ ☐ SUCCESS!

_____ ☐ SUCCESS!

_____ ☐ SUCCESS!

NEEDS WORK

REASONS TO KEEP GOING

DATE _____

> "If you want to have more joy and more wealth than most people do, you have to live more excellently than they do."

TODAY'S GOALS

_____ ☐ SUCCESS!

_____ ☐ SUCCESS!

_____ ☐ SUCCESS!

_____ ☐ SUCCESS!

NEEDS WORK	REASONS TO KEEP GOING

DATE _____

_____ DAYS WITH A WIN!

> "Work keeps us from three evils: boredom, vice, and poverty."
> **VOLTAIRE**

TODAY'S GOALS

_____ ☐ SUCCESS!

_____ ☐ SUCCESS!

_____ ☐ SUCCESS!

_____ ☐ SUCCESS!

NEEDS WORK

REASONS TO KEEP GOING

"Hope is the fuel that when ignited turns you, the rocket, loose with intensity, and all the while accountability is your guidance system that will keep you between the ditches."

TODAY'S GOALS

_____ ☐ SUCCESS!

_____ ☐ SUCCESS!

_____ ☐ SUCCESS!

_____ ☐ SUCCESS!

NEEDS WORK	REASONS TO KEEP GOING

DATE _____

_____ DAYS WITH A WIN!

> "You don't
> have time or
> brain power
> to worry when
> you are focused
> on work."

TODAY'S GOALS

_____ ☐ SUCCESS!

_____ ☐ SUCCESS!

_____ ☐ SUCCESS!

_____ ☐ SUCCESS!

NEEDS WORK

REASONS TO KEEP GOING

DATE _____

"God answers
all prayers. His
answer can be yes,
or no, or grow."
CHUCK SWINDOLL

TODAY'S GOALS

_____ ☐ SUCCESS!

_____ ☐ SUCCESS!

_____ ☐ SUCCESS!

_____ ☐ SUCCESS!

NEEDS WORK

REASONS TO KEEP GOING

"Values matter because having principles you live by brings you joy, peace, and yes, even wealth."

TODAY'S GOALS

_____ ☐ SUCCESS!

_____ ☐ SUCCESS!

_____ ☐ SUCCESS!

_____ ☐ SUCCESS!

NEEDS WORK

REASONS TO KEEP GOING

> "Discipline
> understands that
> the best way to
> get rich quick is
> to get rich slow."

TODAY'S GOALS

_____ ☐ SUCCESS!

_____ ☐ SUCCESS!

_____ ☐ SUCCESS!

_____ ☐ SUCCESS!

NEEDS WORK	REASONS TO KEEP GOING

DATE _____

_____ DAYS WITH A WIN!

"Discipline is the
middle name of
the wealthy."

TODAY'S GOALS

_____ ☐ SUCCESS!

_____ ☐ SUCCESS!

_____ ☐ SUCCESS!

_____ ☐ SUCCESS!

NEEDS WORK

REASONS TO KEEP GOING

DATE _____

> "The thing that moves or motivates us is ... disturbance or dissonance."

TODAY'S GOALS

_____ ☐ SUCCESS!

_____ ☐ SUCCESS!

_____ ☐ SUCCESS!

_____ ☐ SUCCESS!

NEEDS WORK	REASONS TO KEEP GOING

DATE _____ _____ DAYS WITH A WIN!

> "Teaching your children to work is one of the best gifts a loving parent can give."

TODAY'S GOALS

_____ ☐ SUCCESS!

_____ ☐ SUCCESS!

_____ ☐ SUCCESS!

_____ ☐ SUCCESS!

NEEDS WORK

REASONS TO KEEP GOING

> "[TV sets] are stealing our quality time. They are not evil and you can tell by my familiarity that they are in our home; but we are not afraid to turn them off—nor should you be."

TODAY'S GOALS

_____ ☐ SUCCESS!

_____ ☐ SUCCESS!

_____ ☐ SUCCESS!

_____ ☐ SUCCESS!

NEEDS WORK

REASONS TO KEEP GOING

"The best time
to plant an oak
tree is twenty
years ago,
the next best
time is now."
DAVID CHILTON

TODAY'S GOALS

_____ ☐ SUCCESS!

_____ ☐ SUCCESS!

_____ ☐ SUCCESS!

_____ ☐ SUCCESS!

NEEDS WORK

REASONS TO KEEP GOING

> "Finger-pointing, blame-shifting, and whining, while they appear to have merit, are not doing something."

TODAY'S GOALS

_____ ☐ SUCCESS!

_____ ☐ SUCCESS!

_____ ☐ SUCCESS!

_____ ☐ SUCCESS!

NEEDS WORK

REASONS TO KEEP GOING

DATE _____   _____ DAYS WITH A WIN!

> "There is also real delight when you get to earn money with the sweat of your brow and then use that money to help others by giving."

TODAY'S GOALS

_____ ☐ SUCCESS!
_____ ☐ SUCCESS!
_____ ☐ SUCCESS!
_____ ☐ SUCCESS!

NEEDS WORK

REASONS TO KEEP GOING

DATE _____ _____ DAYS WITH A WIN!

> "[W]hen it comes to the people we love, love is spelled *T-I-M-E*."
> GARY SMALLEY

TODAY'S GOALS

_____ ☐ SUCCESS!

_____ ☐ SUCCESS!

_____ ☐ SUCCESS!

_____ ☐ SUCCESS!

NEEDS WORK

REASONS TO KEEP GOING

DATE _____ _____ DAYS WITH A WIN!

TODAY'S GOALS

_____ ☐ SUCCESS!

_____ ☐ SUCCESS!

_____ ☐ SUCCESS!

_____ ☐ SUCCESS!

NEEDS WORK

REASONS TO KEEP GOING

DATE _____

> "You'll never
> leave where you
> are, until you
> decide where
> you'd rather be."
> LEWIS DUNNINGTON

TODAY'S GOALS

_____ ☐ SUCCESS!

_____ ☐ SUCCESS!

_____ ☐ SUCCESS!

_____ ☐ SUCCESS!

NEEDS WORK

REASONS TO KEEP GOING

"Teaching your children to work is also a way of building a meaningful relationship with them, one that will last for years and years—and long beyond the 'injustice' of having to do chores."

TODAY'S GOALS

_____ ☐ SUCCESS!

_____ ☐ SUCCESS!

_____ ☐ SUCCESS!

_____ ☐ SUCCESS!

NEEDS WORK

REASONS TO KEEP GOING

DATE _____

> "When you are diligent over a long period of time you are guaranteed to become wealthy and have more than enough in all areas of your life."

TODAY'S GOALS

_____ ☐ SUCCESS!

_____ ☐ SUCCESS!

_____ ☐ SUCCESS!

_____ ☐ SUCCESS!

NEEDS WORK	REASONS TO KEEP GOING

DATE _____

"Real power
is gentle, not
boastful or rowdy
like a teenager in
a car with a big
engine.... [It is]
becoming what
God intended
you to be."

TODAY'S GOALS

_____ ☐ SUCCESS!

_____ ☐ SUCCESS!

_____ ☐ SUCCESS!

_____ ☐ SUCCESS!

NEEDS WORK

REASONS TO KEEP GOING

DATE _____

"Patience that
is the fruit of
endurance gives
you an increased
ability to respond
to life, rather
than react to it."

TODAY'S GOALS

_____ ☐ SUCCESS!

_____ ☐ SUCCESS!

_____ ☐ SUCCESS!

_____ ☐ SUCCESS!

NEEDS WORK

REASONS TO KEEP GOING

DATE _____

_____ DAYS WITH A WIN!

> "He with the most toys when he dies is dead."
> BUMPER STICKER

TODAY'S GOALS

_____ ☐ SUCCESS!

_____ ☐ SUCCESS!

_____ ☐ SUCCESS!

_____ ☐ SUCCESS!

NEEDS WORK

REASONS TO KEEP GOING

DATE _____   _____ DAYS WITH A WIN!

"In our macho, hyper culture, we've mistaken contentment for weakness, rather than seeing it for what it really is: born of strength."

TODAY'S GOALS

_____ ☐ SUCCESS!

_____ ☐ SUCCESS!

_____ ☐ SUCCESS!

_____ ☐ SUCCESS!

NEEDS WORK	REASONS TO KEEP GOING

DATE _____   _____ DAYS WITH A WIN!

"When bad stuff
happens, resist
the human urge
to blame and
instead join the
elite group called
the doers."

TODAY'S GOALS

_____ ☐ SUCCESS!

_____ ☐ SUCCESS!

_____ ☐ SUCCESS!

_____ ☐ SUCCESS!

NEEDS WORK

REASONS TO KEEP GOING

DATE _____

_____ DAYS WITH A WIN!

> "Work is doing it. Discipline is doing it every day. Diligence is doing it well every day."

TODAY'S GOALS

_____ ☐ SUCCESS!

_____ ☐ SUCCESS!

_____ ☐ SUCCESS!

_____ ☐ SUCCESS!

NEEDS WORK

REASONS TO KEEP GOING

"A valid attempt
that fails is
different from
a life full of
get-rich-quick
schemes that
didn't work."

TODAY'S GOALS

_____ ☐ SUCCESS!

_____ ☐ SUCCESS!

_____ ☐ SUCCESS!

_____ ☐ SUCCESS!

NEEDS WORK

REASONS TO KEEP GOING

DATE _____

> "Courage born of wisdom is powerful courage, not just simple bravery, but deeply held real courage."

TODAY'S GOALS

_____ ☐ SUCCESS!

_____ ☐ SUCCESS!

_____ ☐ SUCCESS!

_____ ☐ SUCCESS!

NEEDS WORK

REASONS TO KEEP GOING

DATE _____ _____ DAYS WITH A WIN!

"When someone recognizes a way to get more pleasure or avoid pain, they are moved, motivated, in that direction."

TODAY'S GOALS

_____ ☐ SUCCESS!

_____ ☐ SUCCESS!

_____ ☐ SUCCESS!

_____ ☐ SUCCESS!

NEEDS WORK

REASONS TO KEEP GOING

DATE _____   _____ DAYS WITH A WIN!

> "If we are desperate enough, sometimes we think shortcuts are okay."

TODAY'S GOALS

_____ ☐ SUCCESS!

_____ ☐ SUCCESS!

_____ ☐ SUCCESS!

_____ ☐ SUCCESS!

NEEDS WORK

REASONS TO KEEP GOING

_____ DAYS WITH A WIN!

> "You have more
> than enough
> only when you
> give it away."

TODAY'S GOALS

_____ ☐ SUCCESS!

_____ ☐ SUCCESS!

_____ ☐ SUCCESS!

_____ ☐ SUCCESS!

NEEDS WORK

REASONS TO KEEP GOING

DATE _____

"Patience born
of maturity will
make you rich.
It will make you
rich in dollars
and rich in
relationships."

TODAY'S GOALS

_____ ☐ SUCCESS!

_____ ☐ SUCCESS!

_____ ☐ SUCCESS!

_____ ☐ SUCCESS!

NEEDS WORK

REASONS TO KEEP GOING

DATE _____

"There is no question that quality time is what is needed to develop strong fruitful relationships."

TODAY'S GOALS

_____ ☐ SUCCESS!

_____ ☐ SUCCESS!

_____ ☐ SUCCESS!

_____ ☐ SUCCESS!

NEEDS WORK

REASONS TO KEEP GOING

DATE _____

> "Contentment can be gathered again when we learn to slow down and count life's simple pleasures."

TODAY'S GOALS

_____ ☐ SUCCESS!

_____ ☐ SUCCESS!

_____ ☐ SUCCESS!

_____ ☐ SUCCESS!

NEEDS WORK

REASONS TO KEEP GOING

> "Without courage, all other virtues lose their meaning."
> SIR WINSTON CHURCHILL

TODAY'S GOALS

_____ ☐ SUCCESS!

_____ ☐ SUCCESS!

_____ ☐ SUCCESS!

_____ ☐ SUCCESS!

NEEDS WORK

REASONS TO KEEP GOING

> "When you teach diligence to children, you are teaching them to have vision and to think long term."

TODAY'S GOALS

_____ ☐ SUCCESS!

_____ ☐ SUCCESS!

_____ ☐ SUCCESS!

_____ ☐ SUCCESS!

NEEDS WORK

REASONS TO KEEP GOING

> "Use the joy
> and peace you
> receive from your
> blessings to give
> you the energy and
> motivation to tackle
> your worries."

TODAY'S GOALS

_____ ☐ SUCCESS!

_____ ☐ SUCCESS!

_____ ☐ SUCCESS!

_____ ☐ SUCCESS!

NEEDS WORK

REASONS TO KEEP GOING

DATE _____

> "The heart of someone . . . who thinks get-rich-schemes will work for them is the heart of a cheater."

TODAY'S GOALS

_____ ☐ SUCCESS!

_____ ☐ SUCCESS!

_____ ☐ SUCCESS!

_____ ☐ SUCCESS!

NEEDS WORK

REASONS TO KEEP GOING

DATE _____

"You find
[contentment]
by learning from
your situation and
fighting through
it to make your
character change
and learning to win
wherever you are."

TODAY'S GOALS

_____ ☐ SUCCESS!

_____ ☐ SUCCESS!

_____ ☐ SUCCESS!

_____ ☐ SUCCESS!

NEEDS WORK

REASONS TO KEEP GOING

DATE _____

> "Giving is an amazing process because it violates common sense, which tells us if we let go we will have less, not more."

TODAY'S GOALS

_____ ☐ SUCCESS!

_____ ☐ SUCCESS!

_____ ☐ SUCCESS!

_____ ☐ SUCCESS!

NEEDS WORK	REASONS TO KEEP GOING

_____ DAYS WITH A WIN!

> "You can't shake hands with a clenched fist."
> GOLDA MEIER

TODAY'S GOALS

_____ ☐ SUCCESS!

_____ ☐ SUCCESS!

_____ ☐ SUCCESS!

_____ ☐ SUCCESS!

NEEDS WORK

REASONS TO KEEP GOING

"We all know
that wealth is not
a way to tell for
sure that someone
is wise, but we
have all made the
mistake of thinking
that wealth is
more important
than wisdom."

TODAY'S GOALS

_____ ☐ SUCCESS!

_____ ☐ SUCCESS!

_____ ☐ SUCCESS!

_____ ☐ SUCCESS!

NEEDS WORK	REASONS TO KEEP GOING

"Surplus wealth
is a sacred
trust which its
possessor is bound
to administer in
his lifetime for
the good of the
community."
ANDREW CARNEGIE

TODAY'S GOALS

_____ ☐ SUCCESS!

_____ ☐ SUCCESS!

_____ ☐ SUCCESS!

_____ ☐ SUCCESS!

NEEDS WORK

REASONS TO KEEP GOING

DATE _____

> "You are made in God's image, and He is a giver; that means in order for you to be all you can be, you must be a giver, too."

TODAY'S GOALS

_____ ☐ SUCCESS!

_____ ☐ SUCCESS!

_____ ☐ SUCCESS!

_____ ☐ SUCCESS!

NEEDS WORK	REASONS TO KEEP GOING

"When you give of yourself you can't help but be lifted up and energized to fight your own problems."

TODAY'S GOALS

_____ ☐ SUCCESS!

_____ ☐ SUCCESS!

_____ ☐ SUCCESS!

_____ ☐ SUCCESS!

NEEDS WORK

REASONS TO KEEP GOING

DATE _____   _____ DAYS WITH A WIN!

"After twenty years of studying millionaires across a wide spectrum of industries, we have concluded that the character of the business owner is more important in predicting his level of wealth than the classification of his business."
DR. THOMAS J. STANLEY

TODAY'S GOALS

_____ ☐ SUCCESS!

_____ ☐ SUCCESS!

_____ ☐ SUCCESS!

_____ ☐ SUCCESS!

NEEDS WORK

REASONS TO KEEP GOING

DATE _____

"The people who are the happiest and the wealthiest got that way by giving."

TODAY'S GOALS

_____ ☐ SUCCESS!

_____ ☐ SUCCESS!

_____ ☐ SUCCESS!

_____ ☐ SUCCESS!

NEEDS WORK	REASONS TO KEEP GOING

DATE _____

"We have exchanged the old layaway pay-until-paid plan for a new credit card 'lay-awake' plan."

TODAY'S GOALS

_____ ☐ SUCCESS!

_____ ☐ SUCCESS!

_____ ☐ SUCCESS!

_____ ☐ SUCCESS!

NEEDS WORK

REASONS TO KEEP GOING

"Hate is not the
opposite of love;
apathy is."

TODAY'S GOALS

_____ ☐ SUCCESS!

_____ ☐ SUCCESS!

_____ ☐ SUCCESS!

_____ ☐ SUCCESS!

NEEDS WORK	REASONS TO KEEP GOING

DATE _____

> "Patience knows that one definition of maturity is learning to delay pleasure."

TODAY'S GOALS

_____ ☐ SUCCESS!

_____ ☐ SUCCESS!

_____ ☐ SUCCESS!

_____ ☐ SUCCESS!

NEEDS WORK	REASONS TO KEEP GOING

DATE _____

> "When you give expecting, you are selfish, and that does not bring you more money or better relationships."

TODAY'S GOALS

_____ ☐ SUCCESS!

_____ ☐ SUCCESS!

_____ ☐ SUCCESS!

_____ ☐ SUCCESS!

NEEDS WORK

REASONS TO KEEP GOING

DATE _____

DAYS WITH A WIN!

> "If the two of you [spouses] aren't in harmony with your money, you aren't really in harmony at all."

TODAY'S GOALS

_____ ☐ SUCCESS!

_____ ☐ SUCCESS!

_____ ☐ SUCCESS!

_____ ☐ SUCCESS!

NEEDS WORK	REASONS TO KEEP GOING

> "Patience allows you to keep your wealth because it makes you decide what something is worth to you."

TODAY'S GOALS

_____ ☐ SUCCESS!

_____ ☐ SUCCESS!

_____ ☐ SUCCESS!

_____ ☐ SUCCESS!

NEEDS WORK	REASONS TO KEEP GOING

DATE _____

> "No one would remember the Good Samaritan if he only had good intentions. He had money as well."
> MARGARET THATCHER

TODAY'S GOALS

_____ ☐ SUCCESS!

_____ ☐ SUCCESS!

_____ ☐ SUCCESS!

_____ ☐ SUCCESS!

NEEDS WORK

REASONS TO KEEP GOING

DATE _____

> "Life is an exciting business, and most exciting when it is lived for others."
>
> **HELEN KELLER**

TODAY'S GOALS

_____ ☐ SUCCESS!

_____ ☐ SUCCESS!

_____ ☐ SUCCESS!

_____ ☐ SUCCESS!

NEEDS WORK

REASONS TO KEEP GOING

DATE _____

"We are so
marketed to that
we have started to
believe that more
stuff will make
us happy. But in
this country, more
stuff has resulted
in more debt."

TODAY'S GOALS

_____ ☐ SUCCESS!

_____ ☐ SUCCESS!

_____ ☐ SUCCESS!

_____ ☐ SUCCESS!

NEEDS WORK

REASONS TO KEEP GOING

"Connection, strong connection, takes time and lots of being very real."

TODAY'S GOALS

_____ ☐ SUCCESS!

_____ ☐ SUCCESS!

_____ ☐ SUCCESS!

_____ ☐ SUCCESS!

NEEDS WORK

REASONS TO KEEP GOING

"The fun thing is that when you start to hit some new levels of contentment and peace, you will be catapulted into yet even higher levels."

TODAY'S GOALS

_____ ☐ SUCCESS!

_____ ☐ SUCCESS!

_____ ☐ SUCCESS!

_____ ☐ SUCCESS!

NEEDS WORK

REASONS TO KEEP GOING

DATE _____   _____ DAYS WITH A WIN!

> "Contentment
> is not apathy
> and yet we often
> confuse the two."

TODAY'S GOALS

_____ ☐ SUCCESS!

_____ ☐ SUCCESS!

_____ ☐ SUCCESS!

_____ ☐ SUCCESS!

NEEDS WORK	REASONS TO KEEP GOING

DATE _____   _____ DAYS WITH A WIN!

TODAY'S GOALS

_____ ☐ SUCCESS!

_____ ☐ SUCCESS!

_____ ☐ SUCCESS!

_____ ☐ SUCCESS!

NEEDS WORK

REASONS TO KEEP GOING

"Giving shows strength, perspective, maturity, and a noble selflessness that has become rare."

TODAY'S GOALS

_____ ☐ SUCCESS!

_____ ☐ SUCCESS!

_____ ☐ SUCCESS!

_____ ☐ SUCCESS!

NEEDS WORK

REASONS TO KEEP GOING

DATE _____   _____ DAYS WITH A WIN!

> "Patience is having the nobility to wait because the result is more important than personal pleasure."

TODAY'S GOALS

_____ ☐ SUCCESS!

_____ ☐ SUCCESS!

_____ ☐ SUCCESS!

_____ ☐ SUCCESS!

NEEDS WORK

REASONS TO KEEP GOING

DATE _____   _____ DAYS WITH A WIN!

"All you can do
is all you can
do, and that
is enough."
ART WILLIAMS

TODAY'S GOALS

_____ ☐ SUCCESS!

_____ ☐ SUCCESS!

_____ ☐ SUCCESS!

_____ ☐ SUCCESS!

NEEDS WORK

REASONS TO KEEP GOING

DATE _____   _____ DAYS WITH A WIN!

"We used to be
a country that
admired diligence,
thrift, and integrity.
What we must
remember is that
money allows
us the leverage
to do good."

TODAY'S GOALS

_____ ☐ SUCCESS!

_____ ☐ SUCCESS!

_____ ☐ SUCCESS!

_____ ☐ SUCCESS!

NEEDS WORK	REASONS TO KEEP GOING

_____ DAYS WITH A WIN!

> "In quietness and
> in confidence
> shall be your
> strength."
> ISAIAH 30:15 (KJV)

TODAY'S GOALS

_____ ☐ SUCCESS!

_____ ☐ SUCCESS!

_____ ☐ SUCCESS!

_____ ☐ SUCCESS!

NEEDS WORK	REASONS TO KEEP GOING

DATE _____

> "I don't know what your destiny will be, but one thing I know; the only ones among you who will be really happy are those who will have sought and found how to serve."
> ALBERT SCHWEITZER

TODAY'S GOALS

_____ ☐ SUCCESS!

_____ ☐ SUCCESS!

_____ ☐ SUCCESS!

_____ ☐ SUCCESS!

NEEDS WORK

REASONS TO KEEP GOING

"If you don't like where you are, you have to change what you have been doing. And that takes intensity."

TODAY'S GOALS

_____ ☐ SUCCESS!

_____ ☐ SUCCESS!

_____ ☐ SUCCESS!

_____ ☐ SUCCESS!

NEEDS WORK

REASONS TO KEEP GOING

DATE _____   _____ DAYS WITH A WIN!

> "Never fear that the fire can be too hot because [God] has his hand on the thermostat."

TODAY'S GOALS

_____ ☐ SUCCESS!

_____ ☐ SUCCESS!

_____ ☐ SUCCESS!

_____ ☐ SUCCESS!

NEEDS WORK	REASONS TO KEEP GOING

DATE _____

_____ DAYS WITH A WIN!

"Over the long
term you get what
you deserve, and
none of us like it
when what we
deserve is pain."

TODAY'S GOALS

_____ ☐ SUCCESS!

_____ ☐ SUCCESS!

_____ ☐ SUCCESS!

_____ ☐ SUCCESS!

NEEDS WORK

REASONS TO KEEP GOING

DATE _____   _____ DAYS WITH A WIN!

> "The happiest
> and most joyful
> people are those
> who give money
> and serve.... We
> serve and give our
> way into true joy."

TODAY'S GOALS

_____ ☐ SUCCESS!

_____ ☐ SUCCESS!

_____ ☐ SUCCESS!

_____ ☐ SUCCESS!

NEEDS WORK	REASONS TO KEEP GOING

"Those with the most power in the patience category seem to endure with the most class and with the most ease."

TODAY'S GOALS

_____ ☐ SUCCESS!

_____ ☐ SUCCESS!

_____ ☐ SUCCESS!

_____ ☐ SUCCESS!

NEEDS WORK

REASONS TO KEEP GOING

DATE _____

> "There is no shortcut to any place that is worth going."
> BEVERLY SILLS

TODAY'S GOALS

_____ ☐ SUCCESS!

_____ ☐ SUCCESS!

_____ ☐ SUCCESS!

_____ ☐ SUCCESS!

NEEDS WORK

REASONS TO KEEP GOING

DATE _____

"Marketing has entered our homes and has stolen our peace."

TODAY'S GOALS

_____ ☐ SUCCESS!

_____ ☐ SUCCESS!

_____ ☐ SUCCESS!

_____ ☐ SUCCESS!

NEEDS WORK

REASONS TO KEEP GOING

DATE _____   _____ DAYS WITH A WIN!

> "You must pay the price if you want to secure the blessing."
> ANDREW JACKSON

TODAY'S GOALS

_____ ☐ SUCCESS!

_____ ☐ SUCCESS!

_____ ☐ SUCCESS!

_____ ☐ SUCCESS!

NEEDS WORK	REASONS TO KEEP GOING

> "Being powerful is like being a lady. If you have to tell people you are, you aren't."
>
> MARGARET THATCHER

TODAY'S GOALS

_____ ☐ SUCCESS!

_____ ☐ SUCCESS!

_____ ☐ SUCCESS!

_____ ☐ SUCCESS!

NEEDS WORK

REASONS TO KEEP GOING

"You will seldom meet someone with patience rooted in power who has not seen heavy trials."

TODAY'S GOALS

_____ ☐ SUCCESS!

_____ ☐ SUCCESS!

_____ ☐ SUCCESS!

_____ ☐ SUCCESS!

NEEDS WORK	REASONS TO KEEP GOING

> "Contentment is more than things, or stuff; it's your ability to cope with and deal with your situation and circumstances."
>
> **SHARON RAMSEY**

TODAY'S GOALS

_____ ☐ SUCCESS!

_____ ☐ SUCCESS!

_____ ☐ SUCCESS!

_____ ☐ SUCCESS!

NEEDS WORK

REASONS TO KEEP GOING

DATE _____

> "Teaching your children how to use their money responsibly means teaching them to save."

TODAY'S GOALS

_____ ☐ SUCCESS!

_____ ☐ SUCCESS!

_____ ☐ SUCCESS!

_____ ☐ SUCCESS!

NEEDS WORK	REASONS TO KEEP GOING

DATE _____

_____ DAYS WITH A WIN!

> "Blessed is the man who finds wisdom, the man who gains understanding."
> PROVERBS 3:13 (NIV)

TODAY'S GOALS

_____ ☐ SUCCESS!

_____ ☐ SUCCESS!

_____ ☐ SUCCESS!

_____ ☐ SUCCESS!

NEEDS WORK	REASONS TO KEEP GOING

DATE _____   _____ DAYS WITH A WIN!

> "Work like it all depends on you and pray like it all depends on God."
> ST. AMBROSE

TODAY'S GOALS

_____ ☐ SUCCESS!

_____ ☐ SUCCESS!

_____ ☐ SUCCESS!

_____ ☐ SUCCESS!

NEEDS WORK	REASONS TO KEEP GOING

DATE _____

"The depth and
commitment of
your relationship
must match or be
deeper than the
seriousness of
the problem being
confronted."

TODAY'S GOALS

_____ ☐ SUCCESS!

_____ ☐ SUCCESS!

_____ ☐ SUCCESS!

_____ ☐ SUCCESS!

NEEDS WORK

REASONS TO KEEP GOING